Managing Time

Pocket Mentor Series

The *Pocket Mentor* Series offers immediate solutions to common challenges managers face on the job every day. Each book in the series is packed with handy tools, self-tests, and real-life examples to help you identify your strengths and weaknesses and hone critical skills. Whether you're at your desk, in a meeting, or on the road, these portable guides enable you to tackle the daily demands of your work with greater speed, savvy, and effectiveness.

Books in the series:
Leading Teams
Running Meetings
Managing Time
Managing Projects

Managing Time

Expert Solutions
to Everyday Challenges

Harvard Business School Publishing

Boston, Massachusetts

No part of this publication may be reproduced, stored in or introduced into a retrieval system, or transmitted, in any form, or by any means (electronic, mechanical, photocopying, recording, or otherwise), without the prior permission of the publisher. Requests for permission should be directed to permissions@hbsp.harvard.edu, or mailed to Permissions, Harvard Business School Publishing, 60 Harvard Way, Boston, Massachusetts 02163.

Library of Congress Cataloging-in-Publication Data

Pocket mentor. Managing time.
    p. cm. — (Pocket mentor series)
  Includes bibliographical references.
  ISBN 1-4221-0186-X
  1. Time management—Handbooks, manuals, etc. 2. Scheduling—Handbooks, manuals, etc. I. Title: Managing time. II. Harvard Business School Press.
III. Series.
  HF5734.5.P63 2006
  658.4'56—dc22

The paper used in this publication meets the requirements of the American National Standard for Permanence of Paper for Publications and Documents in Libraries and Archives Z39.48-1992

Contents

How to Develop Good Time-Management Habits   63

Implement these useful ideas for developing good time-management habits.

Tips and Tools   69

FAQs   71

Frequently asked questions about managing your time are answered by the mentor.

Tools for Managing Your Time   75

Worksheets to help you plan, implement, and evaluate leveraging your time.

Test Yourself   81

A helpful review of concepts presented in this guide. Take it before and after you've read the guide to see how much you've learned.

To Learn More   87

Further titles of articles and books if you want to go more deeply into the topic.

Sources for *Managing Time*   93

Notes   96

For you to use as ideas come to mind.

Mentor's Message: Leverage Your Time to Manage It

Everyone seems to be frustrated with not having enough time. It always strikes me as funny, because time is fixed and we all have the same amount of it. So, what is the problem?

The reality is that we are really frustrated with one of two things:

- We feel as if we are not accomplishing what we would or should be doing.

- We feel as if we have lost control.

While this guide cannot produce more time in a given day, it can help you to improve your chances of accomplishing your goals and ultimately feel more in control.

There are two key concepts to think about as you explore this guide: **time leveraging** and **time management**. People who are effective at leveraging their time allocate time to the things that matter most, the things that give them the greatest return. Those who leverage their time think critically about how they should be spending it and have a clear plan in mind. Time management, on the other hand, is something most of us have already read or heard about. Time management is about discipline. It's about execution. It's about making sure that you are not wasting time and that you are indeed following your plan.

Bottom line, managing your time is much more than making a to-do list and learning to say to no. It's a skill—a skill that requires self-assessment, planning, and continuous discipline and improvement. The truth is, even those who consider themselves time-management masters get sloppy. So, whether you are just learning to better manage your time or are looking for a new approach to using your time effectively, this guide will help.

Enjoy the guide; after reading it and using the tools provided, you will:

- better understand the importance of time leveraging

- have assessed the way you spend your time and uncovered opportunities for improvement

- have developed a plan for leveraging your time that will bring you closer to accomplishing your goals

- better understand how to manage your time, in particular, how to time-box

- have gained insight and tips through learning about the experiences of others who recognize the inherent constraint of time and have made it a lifelong quest to capitalize on this valuable resource.

The more we learn, the more skilled we'll become, and the better we'll feel about our accomplishments and successes.

Good luck!

Melissa Raffoni, Mentor

Melissa Raffoni is Founder of Professional Skills Alliance, Melissa Raffoni has over ten years of professional experience, working with hundreds of clients ranging from start-up to Fortune 500, with a significant focus on business-to-business services. Prior to starting her independent consulting practice, Melissa played significant roles building Oracle's Change Performance Consulting Practice and *Inc. Magazine*'s Eagles CEO Peer Group Program. She is on the faculty at the Sloan School of Management at MIT and has published numerous articles with *Harvard Management Update.*

How to Leverage Your Time: Assess and Plan

How to Look
at the Big Picture

Dost thou love life? Then do
not squander time, for that's the stuff life is made of.
—Benjamin Franklin

T ime—it's a resource that we can't buy or sell, share with others or take from them, get more of or have less of. Every day, each of us has the same amount of time—24 hours. It's what we do with it that makes a difference. The people who make the most of their time may apply different techniques and systems, but they all have one thing in common. They have a vision of how they want to spend their time, a vision that includes a clear sense of priorities. They know what they want to do with their time.

Peter Wakeman and his wife, Laura, founded the Great Harvest Bread Company 25 years ago. As entrepreneurs, it would have been easy to allow their work to consume every moment of their lives. But they had a vision of how they would spend their time, and one priority was clear from the beginning: They would not work on weekends and they would take a vacation every year.

"In the early days of the business we had simple rules, but we followed them like a religion. One was the two-day weekend. We never violated that, no matter what—it was a line we were afraid to cross, as though lightning would strike us down if we did."

—Pete Wakeman, owner

Great Harvest Bread Company

Since then, the Great Harvest Bread Company has grown to a chain of 137 franchises. Their priority of having personal time drove Pete and Laura to grow their business in a very conscious way. For a pair of successful business owners, Pete and Laura take a surprising amount of time off from work. It's all done with a rigorous attention to leveraging time.

"We really like strong lines between things. We carry time cards, and we punch in, punch out, to the nearest five minutes. We know when we're working. . . . I have a little Excel sheet I keep, and we make a conscious decision each year how many hours we will work. . . . In 1996 we decided to go to 1,000 hours each, basically half-time. . . . Aside from the 1,000-hour rule, we vary our schedule any way we want."
—Pete Wakeman

TIME LEVERAGING *n* **1:** spending your time wisely on activities that move you closer to your goals. **2:** the process of assessing and planning how to use your time to accomplish your goals.

What's the value of leveraging your time?

Whatever your priority is—whether it's personal time, as it is for Pete and Laura, or another goal such as increasing sales, developing a new product, writing a business plan, or completing a project—leveraging time can help you achieve it.

What's the difference between leveraging your time and managing it? Leveraging time is a strategy of using time in an intelligent way to pursue your most important goals. Managing time is the day-to-day process you use to leverage the time—the scheduling, the to-do lists, the delegating, and other systems that help you use time efficiently. Without the strategy—the vision and the plan—time management won't necessarily help you achieve your goals. That's why the first step in leveraging your time is to clarify your priorities.

Why do we do what we do?

Most of us have schedules that we follow, deadlines we meet, tasks we achieve efficiently and competently every day. But why? *Why* do we do the things that we do? *How* do our activities and accomplishments get us closer to our professional and personal goals? Try answering these questions:

- Are you using your time to accomplish the things you truly want?

- Are you simply running in place?

- Are you somewhere in between—moving forward, but slowly and uncertainly?

If you're not using your time to pursue your most important goals, then it's time to change.

Look strategically at the big picture

Time leveraging means looking strategically at how to spend your time. It means making sure you are spending time in the right places—on the things that are most important to you. It means allocating your time so you get the biggest return for the time spent.

For example:

- Do you get more leverage from doing work yourself or from training a team of others?

- Do you get more leverage from reading manuals to learn a new skill or from a few intensive and structured learning sessions?

- Do you get more leverage from your team with an open-door policy or offering support for team solutions?

Simply put, to avoid "running in place," make sure you are leveraging your time appropriately.

How to Audit
Your Time

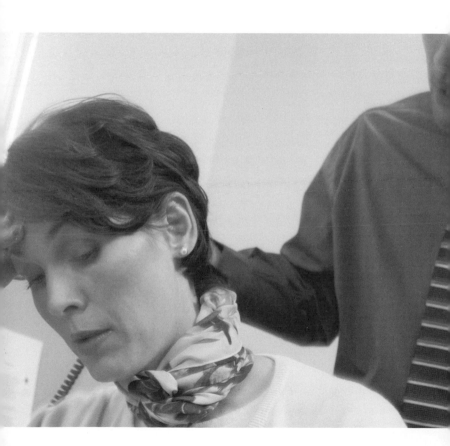

I deally, everything you do should be valuable for you—valuable in terms of actively moving toward your professional or personal goals—the things *you* want to achieve. No one else can make these decisions for you. You have to decide what's important to and for you.

Create a big-picture vision of where you want to be

In this section, you'll learn how to conduct a *Baseline Time-Management Audit* and create a *Current Time Allocation Pie Chart*. You'll then create a *Target Allocation Pie Chart*.

The first phase in leveraging your time is to assess how you are currently spending your time. Although conducting a time audit may seem like busywork, it's actually an important first step in leveraging time. In order to spend time effectively, you need an accurate picture of how you are spending your time now. This information about what you're really doing will help you to create a picture that shows you where you want to be. You'll determine how what you *are* doing relates to what you *want* to or *should* do. As you look at how you are spending your time now, your goals will come into focus more clearly.

Break down your work
into goal-related categories

Here are some typical categories that most managers spend their time on. You may find that your categories differ from these, but the general process of identifying them remains the same.

- **Growth and improvement.** This category focuses on *opportunities*, not crises. It's often the one in which the added value you bring to your unit or company is the greatest. For a product manager, it's the time spent innovating; for an operations manager, it's the time spent improving processes; for the senior executive, it's the time spent on strategy.

- **Managing people.** You may want to break this down into three smaller goals: 1) managing up, 2) managing across, and 3) managing down. Coaching and mentoring direct reports or a team enable you to use your time better, but you must also cultivate lateral and upward relationships in order to be successful. Effective leaders understand that time spent cultivating upward and lateral relationships is high-leverage time that can help you move toward your goals.

- **Nonmanagerial responsibilities.** Most managers have day-to-day responsibilities beyond managing people. For a project manager, it means tracking schedules and budgets and dealing with vendors. For an architect, it may be designing a building. For a software developer, it may mean writing code, or checking everyone else's. Whatever your job, these are the ongoing, daily activities that can be defined as "business as usual."

?What Would YOU Do?

The Fun House

D aniel was giddy after his promotion. He knew his new responsibilities would be challenging, but he hadn't expected to lose control completely. Buffeted about the company by others, dragged in and out of meetings by his boss, his peers, and his direct reports, Daniel's head was spinning. The pile on his desk grew and grew. And every time he'd pull something out of the pile to work on it, someone would need him to do something ASAP, or the phone would start ringing, or an e-mail would pop up on his screen, or another meeting would start.

One evening, he was alone in his office. No people. No phone. No e-mails. Just Daniel and the big pile. He didn't even know where to begin. At the top? That stuff might be the most important. At the bottom? That stuff had been around the longest. Daniel sighed. How had he come to this? He'd been a terrific worker, gotten everything done efficiently and on time, really enjoyed his work. Why was he so out of control as a manager? How could he figure out where to focus his energy? How could he regain control over his own day?

What would YOU do? The mentor will suggest a solution in *What you COULD do.*

- **Administration.** Administration includes such necessary chores as assessing your department's resource needs, interviewing job candidates, responding to letters and e-mails, filling out time sheets and expense reports, and writing performance evaluations. This is the category that shocks most people when they do their time audit. Administrative tasks tend to consume great amounts of time.

Audit your time for one week

Carefully examine and record the time you spend on each activity over the course of one week. This one-week time-management assessment gives you a snapshot of how you actually spend your time. Keeping track of your hours for a week is not difficult, and the results are often surprising.

"The last time I kept a log, I was surprised to learn that when I am in the office, I spend almost half my time on the telephone, either taking calls or leaving messages for people who aren't available."
—Elaine Biech,
   The Consultant's Quick Start Guide

Focus on your most important activities. Rather than covering all your activities, you may want to conduct a single goal audit in a category that is particularly important for you.

For example, Beth Chapman, engagement manager for a healthcare consulting services group, was sure that she was spending too much time on administrative tasks, so she audited the time she spent in that area for a week.

"Since I travel a lot, I have to do a lot of expense reports. I kept a really accurate record of every minute I spent doing expense reports. At the end of a week, I documented that I had spent four hours on expense reports—that's half a day! When I saw the actual numbers, even I was surprised. Then I made a case to my supervisor that a half day of my time with our customers during a one-week period was a lot more valuable to the company than a half day of my time filling out expense reports."

—Beth Chapman,
   engagement manager

Audit your *personal* time as well as your work time. Time management is not just about working more efficiently and getting more done. Time management is a valuable tool that can help you achieve balance in your life. To get the *whole* picture, as well as the *big* picture, audit the time you spend away from work on a separate chart.

Leverage your time to achieve your desired lifestyle. For example, when Elisabeth Choi, an equity analyst and mother of two preschoolers, decided to reduce her workweek from 40 to 30 hours, she found that fixed schedules helped her use her time effectively so she could do the things she wanted to do.

"You want to watch your kids grow up, do yoga, exercise, and work in the garden. When I started working part-time, I began to use a fixed schedule. For example, every Tuesday morning I go shopping. The supermarket is empty then, so it's very efficient. I also learned how long things really took. Once you have a handle on what has to get done and how long those things take, then the rest is free time.

The more you can organize your time, the more time you have to do the things you want to do. It's why you decided not to be out there working full-time and going crazy."

—Elisabeth Choi,
  equity analyst

Steps to Auditing Your Time

To audit the time you spend at work:

1. Create a chart like the one shown on the next page. List the days of the week down the rows. Across the top of the columns, list the major goal-related categories that you spend time pursuing.
2. After you complete an activity, record the time you spent under the related category. For example, after a one-hour sales call, enter the time under the "sales" category.
3. At the end of the day, and at the end of the week, add the total hours spent on each category.
4. Analyze your audit. Divide the total time spent on each goal into the total time spent at work. Translate these numbers into percentages, as shown below.
5. Create a pie chart that visually shows how you have spent your time during the past week.
6. After examining the results of your audit, ask yourself, "Is this how I want to be spending my time?"

The sample chart (Baseline Time-Management Audit Tool) on the following page shows the results of a time audit, including the percentage breakdown shown in the bottom row.

(continued)

Steps to Auditing Your Time *(continued)*

BASELINE TIME-MANAGEMENT AUDIT TOOL

Week Ending: (04/02)	Activity: Sales	Activity: Customer Management	Activity: Team Management	Activity: Strategic Planning	Activity: Managing Up	Activity: Administration	Total Time/Day:
Monday	2 hrs	1 hr	3 hrs	0 hrs	0 hrs	2 hrs	8 hrs
Tuesday	3	1	4	0	0	2	10
Wednesday	7	0	0	0	1	2	10
Thursday	0	3	3	0	0	2	8
Friday	1	2	0	3	1	2	9
Total Time / Activity	13 hrs	7 hrs	10 hrs	3 hrs	2 hrs	10 hrs	44 hrs
% of Time	29%	16%	22%	7%	4%	22%	100%

Administration 22%
Sales 29%
Managing Up 4%
Strategic Planning 7%
Team Management 22%
Customer Management 16%

Tip: Use a calendar or a PDA to track your time— whatever is most convenient.

What You COULD Do.

Let's go back to Daniel's problem.

The mentor suggests this solution.

The spinning-head syndrome Daniel is experiencing can often accompany a promotion into management. But he can catch his breath by taking these three steps:

1. Daniel needs to slow down and start thinking about leveraging and managing his time. First, he needs to determine what his new job entails and break his responsibilities into key goals. Once the goals are clear, he can then figure out what his priorities are in each area. He may need to seek the advice of his supervisor and get input on what is expected of him so he can determine what is, and what isn't, a priority.

2. Once Daniel has a clear picture of how he should be spending his time, he can then start to assess how well he is managing his time. To do this, Daniel could start tracking his time to determine what tasks are steering him off track. This will also help Daniel estimate how long things will actually take to complete, allowing him to plan more accurately in the future. By going through this exercise, Daniel can work with his supervisor to continue to shape his role and get the help he needs, whether it's an assistant or delegating tasks to others.

(continued)

Daniel will most likely also have to start being a bit more disciplined when it comes to sharing his time. If Daniel is respectful of his own time, he will find that others will begin to respect it as well.

3. As for that pile of papers, the first thing Daniel needs to do is skim the pile and organize the material into three smaller (and more manageable) piles:

- Must-do (that is, meeting a deadline or satisfying an important person)
- Can-wait
- Easy-to-knock-off

He can start with the Must-do pile. Then, because it helps build confidence, he can tend to the Easy-to-knock-off pile just to get the work down to a less overwhelming size. Once the Easy-to-knock-off and Must-do piles are out of the way and when small blocks of unexpected time open up, he can deal with the Can-waits.

Compare your audit results to your goals

Once you have an idea of how you spend your time, review your time-audit charts with your supervisor. If you are expected to drive the planning process, but you are currently spending 80% of your time supervising others, your time audit can help you set the stage for an objective, meaningful discussion about your role and what you should be doing.

How to Develop Your Plan

You've identified your major goals, key activities, and associated tasks. The next step in leveraging your time is to make sure your overall plan is realistic and attainable. Put all your high-priority categories and activities together into a Time Leverage Plan and allot time by percent of total time available. How does this percentage translate into actual hours in a 40-hour week? Can you perform the tasks within the given amount of time? (See the table, Time-Leveraging Plan Tool, on the next page.)

Another way to look at the picture is with a pie chart that quickly shows which category should be receiving most of your time and attention.

Once you've created a *Target Time Allocation* pie chart (see figure 1), compare it to your *Actual Time Allocation* chart (see figure 2). How are they different? What can you learn from them?

"Your time audit is important. Your vision of where you should be putting your time—and why—is important. But you need to be proactive. You can't just go in to your supervisor and say, 'Oh, look at this. Do something about it.' You need to present realistic ways to solve the problem, and you need to push to get the resources you need so you can do the job that you were hired to do. Your time audit and your vision of where you want to go are tools that can help you get there."

—Beth Chapman

Week

Goal-related Category	What does success look like? How will I know if I am successful?	% Time Required	Hours/ Workweek	Key Activities
Sales	Close 3 new accounts per month.	30%	12	• Make two sales calls a week. • Research new leads. • Write sales reports. • Submit bids.
Customer Management	Ensure smooth transition from sales to production.	10%	4	• Attend kick-off meetings. • Follow-up with phone calls.
Team Management	• Allot time to meet with staff. • Plan training program for new hires.	20%	8	• One-hour weekly meetings with each rep. Two weekly meetings with team. • Contact Human Resources about new-hire training.
Strategic Planning	Develop new annual strategy.	20%	8	• Draft plan. • Review plan with Joe.
Managing Up	• Keep CEO updated. • Get input from upper management on strategic plan.	5%	2	• Make appointment to meet with CEO. • Arrange two meetings with upper management.
Administration	Expense reports, e-mails, etc.	5%	2	• Deal with e-mails • Review expense reports. • Process invoices.
Other	Contingency time	10%	4	
		100%	40	

Reality-check your actual and target time allocations

When you look at the time it will realistically take to achieve your goals, you may quickly realize that you could end up working 150 hours a week. Everybody needs more time. But since nobody gets more than 24 hours a day, your only choice is to use time more effectively.

FIGURE 1

Actual time allocation

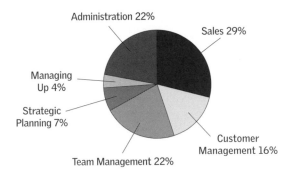

FIGURE 2

Target time allocation

One way to carve out the time you need to pursue your goals is to reduce the time you spend on other activities. But how?

Tip: Be proactive. With documentation about how you are spending your time and a clear picture of your goals, you can take control of your career.

If you've done a time audit of your low-priority activities, you're probably aware of the areas you wish to spend less time on. Now compare the actual time you spend each week with your big-picture time allotment to get a more concrete idea of where and by how much you need to reduce your time.

For example, say you want to reduce by 15% the time you spend on administrative chores—time that could then be transferred to strategic planning and managing up. For most managers, reducing time spent on administrative chores by 15% may be an unrealistic immediate goal, but any steps you take in a positive direction will get you on track.

"Something I've done since high school is make lists. I go out as far as a week. I print out an Outlook calendar for the week. I try to approximate how long things will take and I make lists of phone calls, projects, or other things I want to accomplish that week. By the end of the week, I will have knocked off a bunch of things. I find that in addition to scheduling my time, it just helps me remember what I have to do."
—Elisabeth Choi

How to Manage Your Time: Implement

How to
Time-Box

Leveraging your time takes dedication and persistence, but it pays off when you finally take your plan and put it into action—by managing your time! The key activities in your Time Leverage Plan become your to-do list, making the plan a reality. Some people may start with a "big vision" plan that incorporates all their major goals. Others may feel more comfortable and satisfied by targeting one key goal and starting to work toward it first. Whichever way you start, making a schedule and trying your best to stick to it is an effecttive way of getting there. How can you do this? Try time-boxing.

Time-box a realistic schedule

Time-boxing is a powerful scheduling method that can help you block out your days. With a vision of your big-picture time allocation and task-oriented to-do list to accomplish, you can start to box your time into a manageable schedule like the one shown on page 32. Give yourself a little extra time in your estimates. You're more likely to underestimate than to overestimate how long a task will take. In other words, build in unscheduled time to handle the unexpected.

How to time-box

Simply put, time-boxing is an iterative process that helps you shape your schedule to accomplish your desired goals.

Create a to-do list. Decide what you want to accomplish, and then create a to-do list of tasks. List everything you want to accomplish in a given time period—a day, week, month, or quarter. The to-do list can include goals, tasks necessary to achieve the goals, and personal activities such as exercise.

Break your list into categories. Take your to-do list and organize it by breaking it into categories. Group your tasks by job functions such as strategy, business development, daily operations, and people management. (Remember: the time-boxing technique can be applied to your personal life as well—group a personal to-do list into categories such as gardening, playing golf, or cooking.)

Record your time. For one week, keep a record of what you do and how long each task takes. Track your accomplishments, noting what you finish, what you don't finish. At the end of the week, look back at your record to see if you're spending your time in the right places, the places you feel are important.

Build your time-estimating skill. If you don't set parameters for how much time to devote to each task, to-do lists will only be marginally useful. Estimate how much time you think each item on the list will require. Estimating will not only help you complete the items on your list, but it will improve your ability to estimate time

What Would YOU Do?

Running in Place

arisol went through her pile of "to-do" lists, checking off item after item. Done, done, done, done, done. With each flick of the felt tip, one more task was lifted from her shoulders. Then she copied the tasks that remained onto a new list.

To Do

- Write report for next week.
- Hire new person to replace Tom.
- Meet with Mark to come up with budget for Lawrence bid.

She paused in dismay. These were all the most critical priorities! What had she been doing when she should have been completing these tasks? She glanced at her schedule.

Yesterday there was that meeting with Tony that she really didn't have to go to. Then she and Shelly spent the rest of the morning discussing the office-supply situation. She had a meeting with Lisa to help her with the sales reports. That took the better part of the afternoon. She had done everything she was supposed to do to use her time better—made schedules and "to-do" lists, screened her calls and returned them all at once—and now every one else was going home, and she hadn't even really started! What was the point of all her careful time management when she still was overworked and frenzied?

What would YOU do? The mentor will suggest a solution in *What you COULD do.*

---

and manage expectations of those around you in the future. Think carefully about all the steps necessary to complete the task; set a realistic estimate. This is the step that *"keeps me honest,"* says Beran Peter, CEO of Arkoa, a technical training services company in Westborough, Massachusetts. *"If I realize I'm not going to hit my estimate, I'm able to assess why and evaluate how I might make a change to get back on track."*

Give yourself some wiggle room. Block off the appropriate amount of time on your calendar for each item. For example, if you estimate that writing a business plan will take 32 hours, you could block off four hours each Tuesday and Thursday morning for the next four weeks. The challenge, of course, is prioritizing and fitting the time in where it makes sense. But don't forget to give yourself some leeway. *Overestimate* rather than underestimate. Change is inevitable, and you may want to add tasks midstream.

Tip: Build in time to delegate and shift the balance
of your time from what you are doing now
to what you should be doing.

Tip: Remember that none of these changes will happen overnight, but without a clear vision of where you want to be, they will not happen at all.

As you practice, keep tracking your estimated time against actual time and make adjustments as necessary. Your goal is to manage your day-to-day activities while keeping your big-picture time allocation in mind. (See the table, Time-Box Tool.)

TIME-BOX TOOL		
Adapt this to any type of calendar or software program Schedule for Monday and Tuesday mornings		
Time	**Monday**	**Tuesday**
8:00 a.m.	Task: Research strategic plan. Actual time spent:	Task: Research SP; call Joe. Actual time spent:
9:00 a.m.	Task: Monday staff meeting. Actual time spent:	Task: Follow-up on new leads. Actual time spent:
10:00 a.m.	Task: Plan to delegate invoicing task. Actual time spent:	Task: Meet with Joe about his sales figures. Task: Review résumés for administrative assistant position. Actual time spent:
11:00 a.m.	Task: Return phone calls and e-mail messages. Actual time spent:	Task: Work with Jane. Actual time spent:

"When I want to do something important that doesn't have quite the urgency of, say, an immediate release, I just tell myself I'm just going to spend a half hour each day on it. That's what I do because it will become an emergency if I don't. So each week, on my PDA, I can see if I'm not doing enough future-oriented stuff. I put it on my list and set aside time—every morning from 9:00–9:30—to work on one of those things. It's like practicing the violin."

—Michael Rothman,
    software developer

Tip: Why use time-boxing?

- It forces you to think through your daily tasks and to schedule the time necessary to make them happen.

- It provides a framework for setting expectations and boundaries. If your calendar is full, you'll have to say no—or consciously reassess your priorities.

- It improves your ability to estimate time demands. The ability to estimate how long a task will require is a skill that distinguishes seasoned managers.

- You'll be in a better position to assess—and pull the plug on—unproductive initiatives that consume too much time.

What You COULD Do.

Let's go back to Marisol's problem.

The mentor suggests this solution.

Marisol's dilemma is not uncommon. The root cause could be due to a variety of factors such as: not estimating the right amount of time needed to complete the tasks, procrastinating on the most challenging tasks and opting for the quick hits, or the inability to say no to people who demand her time.

While Marisol should work to uncover the root cause of her dilemma, her first tactical step is to take her to-do lists one step further and begin time-boxing the time she needs to complete her priorities. For each item on her to-do list, she needs to list the amount of time she estimates she will need to complete the task. Then, she can block this time off on her calendar (preferably on a visual tool that others can see).

Once this process is complete, she then needs to train herself to manage "the people-side of the equation." When she is approached, she needs to tell people that her time is booked. She can also make some time in her schedule available to others so they can book time around her already-scheduled time blocks.

With flexibility and persistence, you can make the principles of time-boxing work for you!

How to Manage
Your Time

Leveraging your time takes a commitment to using your most valuable asset to achieve your goals. You may decide to plunge in and work on your whole life—work and personal—at once. Or you may decide to proceed incrementally, working on one category or aspect at a time. Whichever path you take, stay on it. You can't leverage your time without implementing a plan. And that is what time management is all about.

Monitor and evaluate your schedule

As your schedule evolves and delegated tasks begin to fall into place, you should be spending more time on the goals you've established. One way to evaluate your progress is to use the checklist on the page 38.

Your schedule is telling you something. Look at your "sometimes" and "never" answers. Ask yourself why you are not making the kind of progress you'd like to see. Is your schedule realistic? Are your own expectations realistic? How about the expectations of others? What is driving you off course? You may be able to use your schedule to discuss your workload with management.

Look at your "always" and "often" answers. How can you build on your progress to make improvement in other areas?

- Do you feel better prepared and focused?

- Can you make reasonable adjustments to your time estimates?

- Are you making measurable progress on achieving your goals?

- Are you scheduling too many activities?

Tip: Stay focused on your goals. Try to commit to tasks that support your goals. You may be tempted to commit to a task outside of your stated goals to be a team player, but agree to do it only if it does not jeopardize your other work. Learn to say no—diplomatically, of course—to nonpriority projects.

How can you reduce time spent on low-priority activities? Delegate!

Managers are often afraid to delegate, even when they have the resources to do it. But micromanaging can hold you back from achieving your goals, whether those goals are professional or personal.

For example, when Pete and Laura Wakeman, founders of the Great Harvest Bread Company, take off for three-week backpacking trips in the wilderness, they leave their people completely in charge. Pete Wakeman says that delegating is the only way it's possible for them to take a vacation.

"Trust your people, even if they don't solve the problems exactly the same way you do. Problems that may seem to be over their heads usually aren't, and they'll have a much more interesting summer if things are not running like clockwork."
—Pete Wakeman

CHECKLIST FOR EVALUATING YOUR SCHEDULE

	Always	Often	Sometimes	Never
Are you making measurable progress on achieving your goals?			✓	
Do you feel more prepared and focused?		✓		
Are you completing the tasks you set for the week?				✓
Do you have realistic plans for completing tasks you have not finished?		✓		
Are you scheduling approximately the right number of activities?			✓	
Are your time estimates becoming more accurate?	✓			
Can you reduce any activities or tasks that do not support your high-priority tasks?			✓	

Once you've decided what tasks to delegate and you've made the duties involved in that task clear, you have to step back—or forward. For Pete, this literally means putting one foot in front of the other.

"Remember the power of the physical solution: Physically put one foot in front of the other (and I mean your physical foot), and you'll find your physical body moving out the door. Your brain may object vigorously, but it has to go, physically, where your body carries it. Then, physically, don't look back. After a week in the woods or wherever, it will make more sense."

—Pete Wakeman

Steps to Create a Workable Schedule

- Create to-do lists with time estimates.
- Schedule important work or activities that need creativity and intelligence during your peak energy period.
- Don't book every minute. Leave time to deal with crises and the unexpected.
- Combine tasks; for example, open mail while you boot up your computer.
- Determine what time you want to finish work and leave the office. Then proceed backward, putting the most important tasks in your schedule first.
- Identify tasks to work on when you have unexpected free time.
- Keep your schedule easily accessible. Check on your progress throughout the day to see if you are on target.
- Share your schedule with others to reinforce your attention to time management.
- Record your progress.
- Congratulate yourself every time you hit a target!

Delegate creatively

Once you've determined areas where you want to reduce time, be creative about how you delegate. Look for opportunities wherever you find them. Vendors such as financial institutions may provide services that save you time.

> **Tip:** Show appreciation. Administrative assistants and other support staff are often overworked and underappreciated. Make reasonable requests—not last-minute demands. Show that you understand their time is valuable, too. Be polite, supportive, flexible, and return favors.

"The admin is incredibly busy, just like you are. There's only so much you can put on her plate. So when I got a direct-mail piece from a credit-card company offering automated itemized expense reports, I looked into it. I am working with my company to integrate this service into our expense management process, which will save time for a lot of people since many of us use the same card."

—Beth Chapman

Delegate for results

When you delegate, focus on the results, not the process. People approach problems in different ways, so remain open to the variety of potential solutions.

With that in mind, try the following:

- Identify tasks to delegate. In addition to tasks that do not contribute to key activities, consider jobs that other people do better than you can.

- Keep in mind that a job you dislike might be an interesting challenge for someone else. You may hate checking everyone's expense reports. Someone else might not mind a detailed-oriented task.

- Identify the right person for the job. Consider his time, personality, and skill. Even if someone can't do the job as well as you do, a job-training session may be all that is needed to help.

- Communicate expectations clearly, including the requirements for success, time line, and budget. Work together so you both understand what success means. Share relevant information, such as previous research and best practices. Introduce the key people who are involved.

- Delegate authority along with responsibility. Anyone attempting to do a job without proper authority will become frustrated and ineffective.

- Let go. Don't micromanage. Give people the room they need to do the job in their own way.

How to Overcome Obstacles

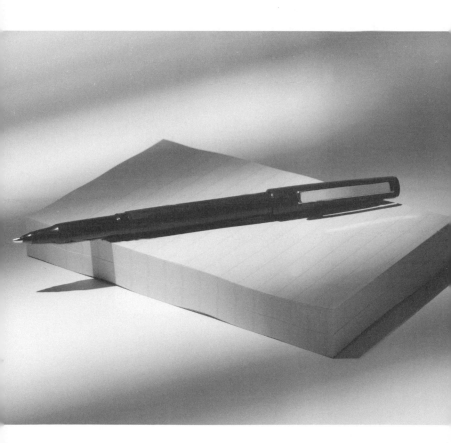

I t takes practice, persistence, and self-awareness to apply the principles of time leveraging and management in your everyday life. As you begin to work toward your goals and adjust your schedule, you'll encounter obstacles that prevent you from using your time effectively. Part of leveraging your time means recognizing these obstacles and working to overcome them.

Recognize common obstacles to managing your time

What sorts of problems are preventing you from leveraging your time? Here are some common difficulties many people have to cope with:

- a chaotic, noisy, demanding working environment

- a poorly organized work space

- a tendency to procrastinate and put off work that needs to be done now

- inefficient meetings and unnecessary travel.

Recognizing the problem is the first step in solving it. Don't feel overwhelmed. Tackle one obstacle at a time. Break it down and keep working on it.

Deal with adverse cultures and working environments

The principles of time leveraging can be adapted to even the most interruption-driven and time-sensitive environments. Through experimentation, sensitivity, and determination, managers in these cultures can learn to leverage their time.

Leverage time in an interruption-driven culture. In many companies, the culture is built on open communications, ongoing teamwork, and a sense of constant, synergistic energy. These environments can be exciting, but they can also be highly distracting. Even if you block out time, there's no guarantee that someone won't pop in or a problem won't suddenly arise. While interruptions can be difficult, managers in cultures like these are expected to be available.

For example, Michael Rothman, a software developer who often works as the tech lead on product releases, has developed several ways to manage his time and be an effective manager.

"Having an open door is a very high priority in the culture of the kinds of companies I work for. You can close your door and people take that as a sign that now is not a good time, but you can't do it a lot."
—Michael Rothman

Another way Michael handles interruptions is to use them to accomplish several things at once. Michael relies heavily on a personal digital assistant (PDA), which he refers to at least 12 times a day. The PDA contains to-do lists for every project he's working on.

What Would YOU Do?

Knock, Knock, Who's There?

Paul wearily turned to his spreadsheets when Carol left. He really hadn't meant to spend the last half hour talking about the company's dental insurance plan, but he was committed to his open-door policy. And it was working. Morale was up. Roland, Paul's predecessor, had been so inaccessible that you'd have to make an appointment with him to tell him that the building was burning down. What a relief it was when Roland was promoted to vice president.

But Paul's accessibility had its drawbacks. He spent all day talking to people, and all night doing the work he should have been doing during the day. He couldn't keep running this chat room. He was becoming exhausted. How could he remain available to his employees and get his work done too?

What would YOU do? The mentor will suggest a solution in *What you COULD do.*

> **Tip:** Progress, not perfection. Your goal isn't
> perfection; your goal is improvement. Every time
> you get a little better at managing your time,
> you move closer to one of your goals.

"I try to synchronize the interrupts. So if someone comes to see me, I determine if what they're talking about is something I can or need to do right away. If it isn't, I can put it on the list. And while the person is in the office, I can pull up the list and go over several things that the two of us might need to talk about, so the interruption becomes a lot more useful."
—Michael Rothman

Michael minimizes interruptions by scheduling regular meetings.

"I have regular meetings, and I really encourage people to defer anything super-important to the regular meeting [if possible]*, which makes the meeting useful. What I want is for them to collect things that come up all week for the meeting, unless it's something that has to be resolved right away."*
—Michael Rothman

Michael wasn't always as well organized as he is now. It took a process of trial and error—and the purchase of a PDA—before he began to work as effectively as he does now.

Review the types of interruptions that tend to occur, and try to develop contingency plans. Then authorize others to deal with the problems if they happen again.

"Most of the time I'm the manager or tech lead, and the nature of the work is very interrupt-driven. I'd usually have eight things I was working on and I'd lose track, and it was frustrating. I'd be working furiously on project C and D for a couple of days, and forget entirely about project A. So I experimented. I had paper lists and other strategies. When I got the PDA, I threw it all away. I have one list. Now, anytime anything occurs to me, anything I have to do, I just add to it on my PDA."

—Michael Rothman

Another advantage of a planning and organizing tool such as the PDA is in helping Michael to manage up.

"One of the nice things about the computer is you now have a list of all the things you did. So on a weekly basis I use that list in a meeting with my manager. If it's something that got checked off the list, it's saved. If you're working on something, it's starred. So at the end of the week, the progress report is already done."

—Michael Rothman

Handle interruptions effectively. You can often delegate the handling of interruptions. But in the cases where you are the only one who can address the interruption, deal with it quickly, so you can return to your priority tasks. Even when handling an interruption takes half the day, focus your energy on the time in the day you have left.

You do not always need to be open for visitors. In some cases, you may find it appropriate to refuse to see a visitor without an appointment.

For example,

- Determine whether your unexpected visitor has an immediate crisis or an issue that has to be dealt with quickly.

- Schedule another time to meet with the visitor, if possible. (You can say, *"I think I can help you, but right now I'm in the middle of something. Can we meet after lunch about this?"*)

- Refer the visitor to another appropriate person, if possible. (You can say, *"I can't pull away right now, but check with Bob and see if he can help. Let me know what the two of you work out."*)

- Make a note of where you are before you break away from your work, and return to that task after the interruption.

If necessary, accept the interruption, take follow-up action, and then recapture your mental position before the interruption. But that's not always easy to do.

Leverage your time in a time-sensitive business

Some businesses are extremely time-sensitive. You must work in the moment almost all day, dealing with customers, answering phones, solving problems. But even in industries such as food services, hospitality, health care, and financial services you can leverage time and move toward concrete goals.

As an equity analyst who follows the stock market during the day, Elisabeth Choi has to synthesize a constant flow of information, opinions, ideas, and news, but, at the same time, she must research stocks and look for opportunities down the road.

"You're looking for bits and pieces of information. All of a sudden, pieces fall into place and you have a picture, but not all the pieces are there. But enough of a picture emerges so you can say 'aha.' It's called the mosaic theory. You're never operating with everything, but you're trying to get enough pieces to reach a conviction. The notes you take when you have conversations, everything you read, all that information that goes into forming the mosaic. By managing your time well, you get more pieces of the mosaic to fall into place."

—Elisabeth Choi

Due to the nature of the stock market, Elisabeth doesn't create a tight weekly work schedule. Instead, she has developed strategies that allow her to snatch chunks of useful time as they pop up. She creates a separate computer file for each stock she is covering. In each file, she enters key information and questions, as well as notes she takes during all the conversations she has about the stock. She is always prepared to leverage the brief, unpredictable time she has with hard-to-reach analysts and company representatives. Each file is a valuable and quick-access reference tool because she can find important details and questions when she needs them.

"These people are very, very busy and they have a lot of competing demands on their time. So you have to be organized and ready to ask questions. You have to be really, really good about taking notes. When I work on a stock, I come up with a list and write out questions about what information I want. Three or four days might go by, and the analyst finally calls back at 2:00 p.m. on Friday afternoon. You quickly pull up your notes or pull up your e-mail. You have the questions right there. And you take down everything you talk about in that conversation, because you're not going to remember it next week or next month. Say you talk to a CFO this quarter; well, you can go back to your notes and then say to him later, 'You said this last quarter; how is it going this quarter?'"

—Elisabeth Choi

A high-pressure, time-sensitive environment can make it difficult to set aside any time at all, let alone time to work on long-range goals. For Elisabeth, organization, note-taking, and discipline allow her to look for chunks of time so she can work on longer-term research.

"When the market's slow, I can take a couple of hours to study a stock I want to decide on in two weeks. And if I have to stop, I take a minute to ask, 'At this point, where does my opinion stand, what is the picture? What are the three things I still don't know enough about to make an informed decision? Do I want to know more about their customer diversification? What does their balance sheet look like? Their inventory?' *I'll make a note in the file that those are the three*

things I want to look at, so when I open up the file next time I know where I left off, and I remember my thought process."
—Elisabeth Choi

Elisabeth's organization saves her valuable time, as well as the time of the busy people she communicates with during the day.

"E-mail has really helped me a lot because I send a list of questions or issues I want to talk about to the company contact or the analyst. If I can't reach them on the phone right away, I can prepare them for the conversation I want to have. I send a quick e-mail about the four things I want to discuss, so they can either respond by e-mail or we can set up a time when I know they'll be there. E-mail helps everyone make the best use of time because we both know what we're going to talk about, and we don't waste time playing phone tag."
—Elisabeth Choi

Deal with disorganized work spaces

For many people, a lack of organization stymies their efforts to use time effectively. There's nothing rewarding about pawing through papers, mail, files, and receipts that are piled up all over every work surface. It wastes time and it's frustrating. Fortunately, there is help for the organizationally impaired (see the table, Office Space Planning Tool on the next page).

> *"Uncluttering your stuff helps you unclutter your mind."*
> —Sandy Block

In her successful business as the Clutter Cutter, Sandy Block helps people organize their work spaces so they can make best use

Category/Item Type	Container and Tips
Bills to be paid	Plastic drawer in a fairly accessible place
Must-do today	An open-top bin. Give yourself easy access in a visible place; empty this bin every day.
Have-to-do soon	A closed-top bin. Monitor this pile carefully to see if it needs subdivision.
To file	Open-top bin. File completed items such as signed contracts, tax documents, and so on that you need once or twice a year or that you need for legal purposes.
Reading materials—journals, newsletters, etc.	Store professional publications that you use as reference materials in magazine holders and place on a shelf near or above the desk where they are easily accessible. Recycle the rest.
Magazines	Put periodicals in a bin on a table or public place so others can read them, or put them in a tote bag so you can carry them to read elsewhere.
Price lists and catalogs	Depending on how frequently you refer to these items, use either closed-top bins or magazine holders. When a new issue or list comes, recycle the old one!
Outgoing items	Place a bin in a highly visible area near the door for outgoing packages, regular mail, or any item that needs to be handed off to someone else, such as a contract that must be signed. Empty it by the end of each day.
Papers for projects	Use a large document box or a cardboard file box for each project or client. When the project is no longer active, store the box in case any material is needed later.
Instruction manuals and warranties	Plastic, closed-top containers are made for this purpose. These documents do not usually need to be highly accessible.
Small items, pens, pencils, stickies, paper clips, etc.	All kinds of containers are made for these items. Drawer separators are also handy.
CDs	Put CDs into CD binders and then store them like books, or use metal mesh CD boxes.

of their time. Sandy has loved to organize space since she was seven years old.

"I grew up in a very messy house and one day a friend walked in and couldn't believe how messy it was, and I was so embarrassed I was sent into a spin, and I've been organizing ever since. In fifth

grade, when I was house-sitting for a neighbor, I organized every room. Just recently, we stayed at [my husband's] cousin's house. I kept looking for the salt, and it was always in a different place, so I completely reorganized the kitchen. I couldn't stand it. I enjoy doing it, but my kids will probably grow up to be messy because I make them be so orderly."

—Sandy Block, the Clutter Cutter

Over the years, Sandy has developed an easy-to-follow system for helping people get organized, and stay that way.

"The biggest problem people have is feeling overwhelmed. They don't feel they have the time to take four hours to organize. No one does that except for people who do it for a living. So don't think you need a four-hour block to get through the process. The first thing you do is realize that you need a place for everything that comes into your office. From there, you can break the whole thing down."

—Sandy Block

"I put serious thought into how to organize the files on my laptop. For example, each client has a file and within each file there are separate folders—such as proposals, deliverables, notes, etc. If I don't need a hard copy (that is, a paper file), I throw it out. Knowing exactly where everything is and eliminating piles of paper has made my life a lot easier. One of my clients, a CEO, noticed what I was doing and has adapted the same technique for himself. We laugh as we carry our laptops around the office, but it really helps."

—Melissa Raffoni,
  Managing Director of Professional Skills

Sandy Block's Seven Steps to Organizing Your Office

1. **Plan.** You need a place for everything that comes into your office. Spend 10 or 20 minutes coming up with a storage plan. What kinds of paperwork do you have? What kinds of bins and storage containers can you put these items in? List the kinds things you need to store and decide where you are going to put them. (Time: 10–30 minutes)

2. **Clear off your desk completely.** (Have a recycle bin, trash can, and/or trash bag handy.) Take everything off your desk and out of your drawers and make one big pile. Clean the desk. This should feel very satisfying. It doesn't matter that everything you have is in a pile now. It's just as inaccessible as it was when it was that big pile on your desk. (Time: 20 minutes)

3. **Do a first-pass throw away.** As you clean off your desk, get rid of as much as you can. You'll save time by having less stuff to store later. Don't get bogged down. Throw away only those things you know you don't want. If you have to think about, just put it in the pile. (Time: 5 minutes)

4. **Shop.** Make a shopping list and remember, there are bins made for just about everything. Go to an office-supply store for most or all of what you need. Art-supply stores also have attractive document boxes as well as containers for pencils, CDs, and other supplies. (Time: 1–2 hours)

5. **Sort.** Put the most obvious items and the things you need immediately into the assigned bins. Put items you use every day in

(continued)

nearby, easy-to-access locations. Be flexible, and remember, you can move things around later. Keep throwing things away as you go. Once you've made a first pass, you'll still have a pile, but your desk will actually be in working order. (Time: 20–40 minutes)

6. Fine-tune your sorting. Pull and sort items from the pile. Now that you have your storage plan, most of the things that you pull from the pile will have a place to go. Throw them out, or put them in their appropriate place or determine a new place. Spend five minutes here and there reducing the pile. (Time: 5–20 minutes)

7. Adjust. At the end of the week, your office may not be perfect, but it is a lot better than it was before. You've made progress. You may find that your to-do box isn't conveniently located or it's too full, but at least you have a to-do box. Keep adjusting according to your priorities. You may need to merge two categories into one, or subdivide a big category into two. Now you have a system, and it's easier to change just one bin than to have to redo the whole pile again. (Time: ongoing, 10–20 minutes as needed)

> **Tip:** Keep receipts, and leave the factory labels and
> price tags on for the first couple of weeks. That way, if
> you find you don't like a particular type of bin, you can
> return it. Label the storage bins with stickies at first.
> When you're sure a container is working for you,
> label it in a permanent way.

Confront procrastination

There's an old joke about the sign taped to the door of the room where the Procrastinator's Support Group meets: *"Meeting rescheduled, come back tomorrow."* It's natural to want to avoid unpleasant work, but the putting-off-until-tomorrow syndrome can present itself in subtle guises—so subtle you may not even realize that you are procrastinating. Some common symptoms of procrastination, along with some suggested solutions, are shown on the following page.

If these solutions don't work, and you must perform the task, do whatever is necessary to get through it, but promise yourself you will do whatever you can to prevent the same circumstances from occurring again. Then follow through.

Avoid poorly planned meetings and unnecessary travel

Everyone has faced the frustration of sitting through a poorly planned meeting or has spent time on the road when it wasn't

PROCRASTINATION SYMPTOM	POSSIBLE SOLUTION
Perfectionism	**Let It Go**
Do you ever find it difficult to complete tasks because you want everything to be *"just right"*? Do you keep redoing things or frequently go *"back to the drawing board"*?	• Learn to recognize that your time is as important, if not more so, than perfection. • Maintain a balanced perspective. Get regular reality checks from coworkers by asking if something is ready to sign off on. Then, when you do sign off, let it go! • Realize your tendency to obsess, and stop yourself. Ask yourself, *"Is this really going to make a difference? Is it worth my effort?"*
Overplanning	**Teamwork**
Do you ever prolong the planning process to avoid beginning work? If you must plan for every contingency, you may find yourself going over budget or throwing off your schedule completely.	Overplanning may indicate that you feel overwhelmed. Work with colleagues and coworkers to tackle the problem and get started. The efforts and perspective of even one other person can often overcome this type of procrastination. Don't be afraid to ask others to help.
Deadline High	**Tighter Scheduling**
Do you ever delay work because you find it stimulating to work against a tight deadline?	An individual contributor may be able to carry off this style effectively, but if you're on a team, this behavior can frustrate other team members, and you may compromise the quality of the job due to lack of time. Work hard to create a schedule and stick to it—especially if others are relying on your contributions or leadership.
Comfort Tasks	**Guidance**
Do you ever revert to tasks you *used* to enjoy and are good at, in order to put off more challenging work?	• You may be avoiding tasks because you are unsure about how to proceed. • Don't be afraid to ask for help from someone who has the skills. Seek advice from a supervisor or a coworker if a task seems too difficult. • Analyze the skills needed to complete the task.
You Don't Want to Do It	**Creativity**
Nothing subtle about this one. You know you are putting it off, and you know why: you don't want to do it.	• Delegate the task to someone who *does* want to do it. • If delegating doesn't work, set an arbitrary start and go from there. • Create a reward for when you finish. For example, if you dread writing a report but you enjoy returning phone calls, write the report first and return the phone calls when the report is finished.

necessary. You may not always be able to control these situations, but there are some ways to improve them.

Make meetings productive for you. A few simple strategies can help you maximize the time you spend in meetings.

- Before you attend any meeting, decide whether you are the best representative. If you do decide it's worth your time, make sure that the meeting has clear objectives and proposed outcomes.

- If you have not received an agenda for the meeting, request to see it in advance. Let others know you cannot send the best person until you know more about the purpose of the meeting.

- Arrange to attend only the part of the meeting that is relevant to you.

- If you are running the meeting, send out the agenda and points to consider before the meeting. This ensures that you maximize all the participants' time and keep the meeting on track. If possible, ask the participants to prepare in advance to improve the effectiveness of the meeting.

?What You COULD Do.

Let's go back to Paul's problem.

The mentor suggests this solution.

Paul needs to meet with each of his employees individually and explain his dilemma. He can make it clear that being accessible is critical to him, but he needs to find a way to get some work done. He should also explain that he would like to learn more about them and how they can more effectively work together so he can help and guide them appropriately. Employees will appreciate the candidness as well as the personal interest Paul is taking in customizing his approach to managing each of them.

He can ask open-ended questions such as:

- What direction, information, or feedback do you need from me to better do your job?
- What do you like or not like about my management style? What could I do differently?
- How would you prefer that we communicate—scheduled meetings? Lunch? Stopping in as needed? E-mail?
- How often and for how long should I expect to meet with you on a regular basis?

After these one-on-one discussions, Paul can make a game plan with each employee. Depending on each one's response, Paul most likely will end up trying for a balance of scheduled and open-door interactions.

Regarding the open-door policy, Paul needs to explore manageable ways to deal with the interruptions and ask the following to get input:

- Is there a certain part of the day when he is more needed than others?
- Can he expect some of the current interruptions to wait until the scheduled meetings?
- How would the direct report feel if Paul closed the door to his office, grabbed a conference room, or came in to the office later if he needed quiet time?
- What is a reasonable amount of quiet time that he should expect to have in a given day?

Now that Paul has communicated the issue to his employees, has a better sense of their individual needs, and has received their input, he can make better decisions about how to manage his time.

Minimize business travel. If you are asked to travel for business, find out if it is necessary to hold the meetings face-to-face rather than via conference call. If the trip is necessary, make sure that you are the best person to make the trip. If not, arrange to have the right person travel instead of you.

When you do have to travel, try to make waiting and in-transit time as productive as possible.

- Organize your materials before the trip, reviewing all background information you may need on the road.

- Take a well-organized briefcase with you.

- Use cell phones and laptops.

- Bring a pile of work or reading or a list of phone calls to make en route.

Take time to avoid or overcome obstacles

All of the problems discussed above can be dealt with by taking the time to do so. Thus, to leverage your time you have to use time. The process doesn't magically occur—it takes a commitment of your time, planning, and resources, but it is time well spent!

How to Develop Good Time-Management Habits

The big picture helps you determine what your goals are and how to move closer to them. Tools such as time-boxing provide resources for putting your use of time into perspective and creating a proactive method for you to leverage your time the way you want to. There are also many simple habits you can develop to maximize your time usage as well.

Manage messages

Most messages today come via the telephone, e-mail, or fax machine. Here are some ways to manage the often disrupting (and occasionally overwhelming) flow of messages.

Develop effective telephone manners. For many, phone calls are a constant interruption. To make the best use of phone time:

- Screen calls using caller ID or voice mail.

- Refer the caller to someone else if possible.

- Keep the call brief and focused.

- Carve out a block of time in the day when you take phone calls and return them.

- When you really need to focus, take work to a room without a phone.

- Use e-mail to accomplish as much communication as possible.

> **Tip:** Handle paper once. Respond
> to it, file it, pass it along, or toss it out.

Steps for Taking Phone Notes

1. Use your computer and your telephone simultaneously. If you often write while talking on the phone, get a headset to plug into the side of the phone. They're not expensive and help prevent neck strain.

2. On your computer, create a separate file for each account, project, or similar category.

3. Before a conversation, list questions you need to ask and information you want to share.

4. Enter the time, date, and people involved in conversation.

5. Write (or enter) the conversation's purpose.

6. List key information received.

7. List follow-up items you and others need to deal with.

8. List items still outstanding.

9. Use logical naming conventions so you can easily access the information within the proper computer folders; for example, a call made to Acme Tech on April 30, 2005 could be coded as 043005Acme_Weekly call.

Use e-mail to save time. E-mail can be just as disruptive as the telephone if you feel the need to open and respond to every message as it comes in. E-mail can be one of the great time-savers of business today if it's managed wisely. The most important e-mail rule is to keep your messages short and simple.

Here are some other ways to make e-mail work for you:

- Ask short, easy-to-answer questions, for example, *"What is the date of your arrival?" "I'd like to contact the caterer you used for your luncheon. Please send the name and number."*

- Keep colleagues, customers, or suppliers updated on ongoing progress. For example, write *"We sent the samples you requested by overnight on Thursday at 4:00. They should arrive Friday before 10:00."*

- E-mail is not a substitute for human interaction. *Do not* use e-mail for messages that may have emotional impact, especially if it's negative, such as, *"I am disappointed in the quality of your report"* or *"I am sorry to inform you that you are being laid off."*

- Alert others to changes that can save time. For instance, write, *"Our 3:00 meeting has been moved from the Fishbowl into Conference Room B."*

- Group several questions together and number them so the recipient can easily copy and reply, answering several items at once.

- Avoid time-wasting missed telephone calls by setting up call dates on e-mail.

- Save e-mails into relevant project files for quick reference later.

Be an efficient e-mailer. Are you an efficient e-mailer? Do you . . .

- use key words in subject lines to give the recipient a clue about the e-mail's content?

- always include your phone number so recipients can get back to you by telephone? (Most e-mail programs have a set-signature function that lets you set up a standard signature.)

- edit your e-mails for brevity and "skim-ability" so the reader can quickly scan the e-mail and take away your main points? Break up text by formatting with white space, headers, and bullet points (such as used here)?

- try to make the e-mail fit into one screen field so the reader does not have to scroll down?

Tip: Straighten up each evening before you leave. It will help you start the next day with a clear mind.

TASKS TO FILL DOWN TIME

5-Minute Blocks	10-Minute Blocks	30-Minute Blocks
Schedule an appointment.	Make a brief phone call.	Skim journals, magazines, newspapers.
Write a quick note.	Outline an agenda for a meeting.	Plan your weekly schedule.
Update your schedule.	Read and respond to e-mail.	Outline notes for a report.
	Plan an upcoming trip.	Fill out an expense report.

Take advantage of unexpected down time. This down time often occurs when you're traveling or when meetings start late. Since this is time that usually can't be used in the pursuit of a meaningful personal goal, use it to be more productive.

Tip: Sort mail while you are going from the mailroom to the office. Toss out junk mail before you even sit down. Immediately sort the rest of the mail into categories, such as *"to-be-paid"* or *"to-do today."*

Tips and Tools

Frequently Asked Questions

What's the biggest problem new managers face in managing their time?

You cannot successfully manage your time if you don't know *how* you should be spending it. The biggest problem new managers face is understanding their goals and priorities. They are not really sure what they should be doing. Because of this uncertainty, new managers often spend time working on the wrong things or let others pull them into activities that aren't directly tied to their priorities and goals. To better understand how you should be spending your time, work with your supervisor to clarify expectations and responsibilities. At the same time, start to get a handle on how long your new responsibilities take so you can better estimate and plan your time as you grow in your new role.

Does it ever make sense to delay important tasks?

It often makes sense to delay working on a task until you have key information or resources. It is also often best not to work on jobs that require sensitivity and clarity of thought when you are upset, angry, or tired. Just make sure that your impulse to delay an important task is not a form of procrastinating.

How do I learn to say no?

Once you've established clear priorities and created a schedule, saying no will become easier. You can set boundaries by explaining your priorities. Rather than putting out fires all day long, schedule a block of time each day to handle issues presented by your direct reports. Then defer all requests but emergencies to that time block. Become disciplined about running meetings, and train reports to recognize issues that can wait until meetings, so they can bring them up then.

Saying no to management can be a little trickier, but you can still use the same techniques. Clearly explain your priorities and the importance of your schedule. You can't always say no when you want to, but if you are firm about boundaries, those times will be less frequent.

What if it is impossible to estimate how long something will take?

Typically difficulties with estimates result from lack of experience with a given task. Regardless of the task, a certain level of time management and estimation needs to be applied to control the costs from becoming unfeasible. Some tasks, such as hiring the right person or following creative pursuits, might seem impossible to estimate, but start by breaking the task down using best guesses. Guess how many people you will need to interview and how long each interview will take. Factor in other time on the pursuit, such as time spent checking references, reviewing résumés, rewriting a job description, and so on. Once you break down a task into its component parts, estimating the total time required will become more obvious.

Another way to estimate a task that you may be unfamiliar with is to ask for help. Find a coworker who is knowledgeable about the job and ask for advice.

The better you become at estimating, the more likely you will be satisfied by your ability to accomplish your goals in the time you set for yourself.

I always forget my initial priorities because I get caught up in the day-to-day matters. How can I avoid this?

Sticking to your priorities is typically a matter of discipline more than anything else. If others constantly interrupt you, you need to lay down some ground rules—ask for no interruptions during a *"closed-door quiet time."* If there is simply not enough time in the day, you need to review your time allocations with your manager and find an alternative solution. A common problem is that you simply have too much to do.

What should I do if I'm spending too much time on something I'm not very good at?

It depends. It's always more comfortable to work on things you are good at, but don't neglect your weaknesses completely. The key is to identify those weaknesses that are inhibiting your growth or success and work on them. For example, a middle-aged sales representative who is uncomfortable with technology will probably have to buckle down and learn how to use a computer in order to stay current.

On the other hand, spending too much time on weak areas that you are not motivated to strengthen or that are not standing in your way can be frustrating and a waste of time. In these cases, you are better off figuring out a *"work-around plan"* and getting back to leveraging your strengths. You will need to judge whether the activities are the ones you want to spend time developing skills for yourself, or whether you need to delegate them.

Tools for Managing Your Time

This sample chart shows the results of a time audit, including the percentage breakdown shown in the bottom row.

BASELINE TIME-MANAGEMENT AUDIT TOOL

Week Ending:	Activity:	Activity:	Activity:	Activity:	Total Time/Day:
Monday					
Tuesday					
Wednesday					
Thursday					
Friday					
Total Time/ Activity					
% of Time					

TIME-LEVERAGING PLAN TOOL

Week

Goal-related Category	What does success look like? How will I know if I am successful?	% Time Required	Hours/ Workweek	Key Activities

Adapt this to any type of calendar or software program

Schedule, Week of _____

Time	Monday	Tuesday	Wednesday
8:00 a.m.	Task: Actual time spent:	Task: Actual time spent:	Task: Actual time spent:
9:00 a.m.	Task: Actual time spent:	Task: Actual time spent:	Task: Actual time spent:
10:00 a.m.	Task: Actual time spent:	Task: Actual time spent:	Task: Actual time spent:
11:00 a.m.	Task: Actual time spent:	Task: Actual time spent:	Task: Actual time spent:
12:00 p.m.	Task: Actual time spent:	Task: Actual time spent:	Task: Actual time spent:
1:00 p.m.	Task: Actual time spent:	Task: Actual time spent:	Task: Actual time spent:
2:00 p.m.	Task: Actual time spent:	Task: Actual time spent:	Task: Actual time spent:

Notes:

**Keep receipts and leave factory labels on containers
until you are sure you want to keep them.**

Category/Item Type	Container	Space Needed
Bills to be paid	Plastic drawer Other:	
Must-do today	Open-top bin Other:	
Have-to-do soon	Closed-top bin Other:	
To file	Open-top bin Other:	
Reading materials—journals, newsletters, etc.	Magazine holders Other:	
Magazines	Magazine rack Tote bag Other:	
Price lists and catalogs	Closed-top bins Magazine holders Other:	
Outgoing items	Bin Other:	
Papers for projects	Document box Size: Other:	
Instruction manuals and warranties	Plastic, closed-top container Other:	
Small items, pens, pencils, stickies, paper clips, etc.		
CDs	CD notebook CD shelf CD box Other:	
Shelves	Dimensions:	

CHECKLIST FOR EVALUATING YOUR SCHEDULE

	Always	Often	Sometimes	Never
Are you making measurable progress on achieving your goals?				
Do you feel more prepared and focused?				
Are you completing the tasks you set for the week?				
Do you have realistic plans for completing tasks you have not finished?				
Are you scheduling approximately the right number of activities?				
Are your time estimates becoming more accurate?				
Can you reduce any activities or tasks that do not support your high-priority tasks?				

Test Yourself

How well do you understand the principles of time-leveraging and time-management?

1. In time-leveraging, what is the driving factor in how you use your time?

   a. The goals of your organization.

   b. Your own most important goals.

   c. Your schedule.

2. You know you are spending too much time on a particular activity and want to make a case to your supervisor for additional resources. In addition to your job description, what else will you use?

   a. Your performance appraisal.

   b. The job description of people to whom you want to delegate.

   c. The results of a time audit.

3. What is the first step in creating a time-management plan?

   a. Break important goals into activities with time estimates.

   b. Create a schedule.

   c. Write to-do lists.

4. How can anyone become more and more effective at scheduling their time?

   a. Keep track of actual time spent on tasks.

   b. Use software programs developed for scheduling.

   c. Reduce time-wasting activities.

5. One way to reduce time spent on low-priority activities is to delegate. Which of the following should almost never be a part of delegating a task?

   a. Giving clear expectations of results.

   b. Granting authority to get the job done.

   c. Ensuring that a precise process for achieving results is followed.

6. Someone comes into your office with a fairly complicated but nonurgent matter that needs input from others on your team. What would be an effective way to handle this interruption?

   a. Make it clear that you are busy and can't talk now.

   b. Ask to defer the discussion to the weekly team meeting.

   c. Call other team members who are involved and have a quick, stand-up meeting to resolve the problem as quickly as possible.

7. Your desk is piled high with all kinds of papers—mail, project information, snapshots, bids, bills. You spend lots of time going through the mess and it's frustrating. Of the following, which is the best way to start getting organized?

 a. Throw nonessential items away.

 b. Create a pile of the most important things you need to do now.

 c. Clear off your desk completely and clean it.

8. What's an effective way to approach completing a task that you don't want to do?

 a. Promise yourself a reward after the task is completed.

 b. Plan to spend as little time on it as possible.

 c. Schedule it for another time.

9. What's an effective way to solve the phone-tag problem?

 a. Be persistent. Keep calling back and eventually you will contact the person.

 b. Call people in the evening at home.

 c. Use e-mail to schedule phone conversations.

10. What's an effective way to handle paperwork?

 a. Sort the paperwork into piles of highest priority, medium priority, and lowest priority.

 b. Always reply right on the paper received rather than create a separate reply.

 c. Try to handle any paper document only once.

Answers to test questions

1b. The time you have is yours to spend, and your own goals, both personal and professional, should drive how you spend it. A clear understanding of what your goals really are will help you leverage your time.

2c. Your job description, combined with the results of a one-week audit showing how you actually spend your time, can make a compelling case for you to get additional resources, or at least re-define your role.

3a. Before you can create an effective schedule or to-do list, you need to determine what activities will help you reach your goals and estimate how much time these activities will take.

4a. As you become better at estimating how long various tasks and activities take, you can create more realistic schedules. By sticking to realistic schedules, you can manage your own expectations about your goals and your progress toward them.

5c. When you delegate, focus on results, not process. People need the latitude to achieve desired results in the way that is most effective for them.

6b. Make team meetings more useful by deferring important but nonurgent issues to them. Over time, team members will begin to use the team meeting more effectively themselves. Simply kicking the person out may be rude, and having an immediate meeting with other members is disruptive to everyone's schedule.

7c. Being disorganized is frustrating and wastes time. Simply throwing things away or creating an in-box pile won't help you solve your problem. Clear off your desk and create a storage plan so you can start to make your office space work for you.

8a. Promising yourself a reward, such as taking a walk or a coffee break after completing something you'd like to avoid, can help you accomplish things you don't like doing and make the job more enjoyable. If you rush through the task, you may not do it correctly. Scheduling for another time is also known as procrastinating.

9c. Persistence may help you get through to people, but phone tag is still a real time-waster for many people. Many people use e-mail to schedule phone conversations. E-mail can also be used to inform people of what the conversation will be about, so the conversation will be as useful as possible.

10c. Try to handle paper only once. Paper pileup can be overwhelming. Have a place to put every piece of paper that comes into your hands, for example a trashcan, an in-box, a magazine rack, an out-box, a catalog storage container.

To Learn More

Notes and Articles

Jim Billington. "Fairly Timeless Insights on How to Manage Your Time." *Harvard Management Update*, February 1997.

Too much literature on time management stresses how to do more faster—essentially how to manage a to-do list. Instead, managers should visualize the end result by "getting on the balcony—seeing the whole field of play and where their undertaking should fit in." Only work that is truly necessary should be done, and the addiction to urgency—fighting fires, fielding calls, firing off memos, and attending irrelevant meetings that can consume a manager's day but add little lasting value—should be avoided. The goal of enlightened time management is to allow people to spend most of their time on work that is truly important, but relatively nonurgent. Work and leisure should both be governed by this same philosophy, because by balancing excellence in work with excellence in relaxation, our lives become healthier and a great deal more creative. A short checklist of practical tips to increase efficiency is included.

John P. Kotter. "What Effective General Managers Really Do." *Harvard Business Review* OnPoint Enhanced Edition. Boston: Harvard Business School Publishing, 2000.

> Controlling your time and highly structuring your schedule can help you boost your efficiency and productivity. But, as Kotter explains, going *too* far in that direction can actually hinder your effectiveness. Managers who limit their interactions to orderly, focused meetings actually shut themselves off from vital information and relationships. Kotter shows how seemingly wasteful activities like chatting in hallways and having impromptu conversations and gatherings can in fact be remarkably efficient. The key to taking advantage of these opportunities? Develop flexible agendas and broad relationship networks. Be willing to respond opportunistically to the events around you—but within a clear framework that guides your decisions.

Hal Lancaster. "Time Management Takes Planning in the Real World." *The Wall Street Journal*, August 19, 1997.

> This article examines why traditional time-management systems have failed. The author describes how many traditional systems do not take into consideration real-world obstacles. He compiles his own list of obstacles and possible solutions.

Dwight Moore. "Managing Message Overload." *Harvard Management Update*, November 1999.

> Getting swamped by a deluge of communications? Moore, an industrial psychologist, explains how to rearrange your

priorities and more effectively manage the many messages that come your way during a typical workday.

William Oncken, Jr., and Donald L. Wass. "Management Time: Who's Got the Monkey?" *Harvard Business Review* OnPoint Enhanced Edition. Boston: Harvard Business School Publishing, 2000.

> Many managers feel overwhelmed. They have too many problems—too many monkeys—on their backs. All too often, they find themselves running out of time while their subordinates are running out of work. Such is the common phenomenon described by the late William Oncken, Jr., and Donald L. Wass in this 1974 HBR classic. This article describes how the manager can reverse this phenomenon and delegate effectively. In his accompanying commentary, Stephen R. Covey discusses both the enduring power of this message and how theories of time management have progressed beyond these ideas.

Thomas J. Peters. "Leadership: Sad Facts and Silver Linings." *Harvard Business Review* OnPoint Enhanced Edition. Boston: Harvard Business School Publishing, 2001.

> Peters suggests that the "sad facts" of managerial life can be turned into opportunities to communicate values and to persuade. The fragmented nature of the executive's workday can also create a succession of opportunities to tackle bits of the issue stream. The fragmentation is precisely what permits a manager to fine-tune, test, and retest the strategic signals being sent to the company.

Peters suggests that the leader must become adept at controlling the process by nudging it in the desired direction.

Kirsten D. Sandberg. "The Case for Slack: Building 'Incubation Time' into Your Week." *Harvard Management Update*, June 2001.

Companies are constantly striving to cut the slack time in their processes. But this zeal for lean operations has led many companies to cut the slack, or thinking time, out of human processes as well. In an era of tight production deadlines—and even tighter margins—how can you be sure to build in the "down time" workers at your company need to generate breakthrough ideas and strategies? Real-world managers and several academics discuss the merits of slack time and offer advice on how to fit this new essential into your business.

David Stauffer. "Making Sense of Your Time Bind, and Escaping It." *Harvard Management Update*, August 1997.

The author focuses on ways to manage the time bind. Using current research, he identifies specific tips for approaching time, setting goals, and scheduling time.

Constantine Von Hoffman. "Getting Organized." *Harvard Management Update*, January 1998.

Although there is no single best method for organizing yourself, this article taps into some perennially useful techniques for managing your disorganization. Through space management, organizing your schedule in collaboration with others, prioritizing your to-do list, and correctly filing things so they remain accessible, managers can reduce the hundreds of hours lost each year searching for lost items.

Books

Jack D. Ferner. *Successful Time Management: A Self-Teaching Guide.* New York: John Wiley & Sons, 1995.

> This book provides a broad overview of the principles of time management. The author maintains that time management is a process that involves analysis, planning, and commitment. He includes exercises and references that can be incorporated into everyday professional and personal situations to help you manage your time successfully.

Julie Morgenstern. *Time Management from the Inside Out: The Foolproof System for Taking Control of Your Schedule and Your Life.* New York: Henry Holt, 2000.

> Those who fear "time management" because they worry about living uncreative or overly scheduled lives will find themselves reassured by Morgenstern's ability to customize her system. The most important thing readers must do, she emphasizes, is to create a time-management system that fits one's personal style—whether it be spontaneous and easily distracted or highly regimented and efficient.

William Oncken, Jr., Hal Burrows, Kenneth Blanchard. *The One Minute Manager Meets the Monkey.* Quill, 1991.

The message in this book is let your direct reports take on the tasks they can and should do. Trust them and train them, but don't do it yourself!

Sources for
Managing Time

We would like to acknowledge the sources that aided in developing this topic.

Elaine Biech, *The Consultant's Quick Start Guide*

Sandy Block, the Clutter Cutter

Beth Chapman, engagement manager, Health Care Consulting Services Group, McKesson Corp.

Elisabeth Choi, equity analyst

Melissa Raffoni, Managing Director, Professional Skills Alliance, Boston, Massachusetts

Michael Rothman, software developer

Peter and Laura Wakeman, owners, Great Harvest Bread Company

Stephen R. Covey, Roger Merrill, and Rebecca R. Merill. *First Things First: To Live, to Love, to Learn, to Leave a Legacy.* New York: Simon & Schuster, 1995.

William Oncken, Jr. *Managing Management Time: Who's Got the Monkey?* New York: Prentice Hall Trade, 1987.

Jim Temme. *Productivity Power: 250 Great Ideas for Being More Productive.* Mission, KS: SkillPath Publications, Inc., 1993.

Alex MacKenzie. *The Time Trap.* New York: AMACOM, 1997.

Melissa Raffoni. "Got a Need for Speed? What You Can Learn from Rapid Application Development." *Harvard Management Update*, November 2000.

Melissa Raffoni. "How to Be Sure You're Spending Your Time in the Right Places." *Harvard Management Update*, October 2001.

Notes

Notes

Notes

Notes

Notes

How to Order

Harvard Business School Press publications are available worldwide from your local bookseller or online retailer.

You can also call
1-800-668-6780

Our product consultants are available to help you 8:00 a.m.–6:00 p.m., Monday–Friday, Eastern Time. Outside the U.S. and Canada, call: 617-783-7450.

Please call about special discounts for quantities greater than ten.

You can order online at
www.HBSPress.org